What Others Are Saying...

"The expulsion process can be a complicated one, but when a student commits an act that requires a hearing, it is an opportunity to develop a plan that can get him back on track with his education. Over the years, I have worked with Mike Mackniak on a number of cases that have done just that. His knowledge of education law, his understanding of the circumstances that led the student to the expulsion in the first place, and common sense have been crucial to a resolution. Mike listens to both the administration and the family of the student and comes up with decisions that are truly in the best interests of both parties."

– Neil C Cavallaro, Superintendent
West Haven Public Schools

"Michael Mackniak is the ultimate professional. He is fair in his decision-making and provides excellent guidance to both parties. He provides equitable treatment coupled with a rational approach for what is best for the student and the school district."

– Jeffrey Burt, Assistant Superintendent
Milford Public Schools

"Working with Attorney Michael Mackniak for the last 15 years, has been a pleasure. As a hearing officer, Attorney Mackniak has a knack for getting to the heart of every case and shows sound legal judgment combined with compassion for students who are in the most difficult of situations. His unique approach is appreciated by administration and students and their families alike."

– Caroly Dugas, Administration Attorney
Berchem, Moses & Devlin

"This manual is a must have for parents and student attorneys. In addition to providing applicable law and policy information, it provides an invaluable glimpse at the inner workings of the impartial hearing officer at an expulsion hearing. This is a great resource tool."

– Marcia Blake, Student's Attorney
The Blake Law Group

"I have attended numerous hearings at which Attorney Mackniak presided as a Hearing Officer. He is organized and impartial in his approach to hearings, ensuring that all parties have a fair opportunity to be heard. At all times, he values the integrity and security of the educational environment, while balancing the rights and unique circumstances of students and families that appear before him."

– Elizabeth Adams, Administration Attorney
Law Offices of Elizabeth Adams

The Expulsion Hearing

An Administrative Guide

Michael Mackniak, JD
Conservative Care, Inc.

The Expulsion Hearing:
An Administrative Guide

Conservative Care Inc.

Copyright © 2016. All Rights Reserved

No part of this document may be reproduced or transmitted in any form or by any means, electronic, mechanical, photocopying, recording or otherwise, without prior permission of Conservative Care Inc.

Requests for permission to make copies of any part of the work should be submitted to the publisher at:

 Conservative Care, Inc.
Michael Mackniak, JD.

750 Straits Tpke, Unit 2c,
Middlebury CT 06762
MichaelMackniak.com

Cover and inside layout design: TheBookProducer.com
Editor: Edward Mackniak
Printed in the USA.

First Printing

ISBN 978-0-9974214-2-2
LCCN 2016942702

The material in this book cannot substitute for professional advice; further, the author is not liable if the reader relied on the material and was financially damaged in some manner.

DEDICATION

I am writing this book for teachers and administrators as a tool that will walk them through the process involved in expulsion hearings and the expectations of that process.

I write it for the parent who most assuredly has not been through this process before and the counselor who is walking through it with a family.

Most of all I write for the students that I have expelled from school in hopes that I was able to impart upon them the importance of their education and the education of their peers. My core belief – and I say it often on the record – is that the expulsion process need not be seen strictly as punitive. These kids will come back to school and we will educate them. We will help their family and their home life to the extent and power we have to do so. And we will do it thoughtfully, planfully and repeatedly until we get it right.

CONTENTS

General Statement 9

1. **CONCEPTS** 15
   Preliminary 15
   Notice 17
2. **LEGALESE** 21
   Exhibits/Hearsay/Helping Student 21
   Evidence 22
   Hearsay 22
   Police Reports 24
3. **CONSIDERATIONS** 27
   Special Education and 504 Accommodations 27
   Request for Continuance 29
4. **THE HEARING** 33
   Recording 34
   Basic Principles of Law 35
       Mandatory Expulsion Hearings 39
       Expulsion for Off Campus Activity 40
       Executive Session 42
       Bifurcated Hearing 43
5. **SELF REPRESENTED PARTIES** 47
   Presenting the Case 47
   Witness Testimony 48
   Cross Examining Student Witnesses 49
6. **THE DECISION-MAKING PROCESS** 53
   Should the student be expelled? How long? 53
   Alternative Educational Opportunity 55
7. **I REST** 59

Appendix A 61
Appendix B 62

GENERAL STATEMENT

I am an Impartial Hearing Officer that is called to sit in the place of local Boards of Education/directors when the administration is recommending to them that a student be expelled from school. This is legal and is codified under the law and, frankly is the most efficient means of resolving expulsions in a timely and fair manner. As an attorney I am uniquely qualified to interpret the laws pertaining to expulsions as opposed to the lay person acting in this capacity.

As an independent hearing officer I must be just that – independent. If you are an administrator, or a student or a lawyer who feels that I should decide cases as anything but independent, then I am not the guy you should call for the job.

I will admit that my propensity is to try to give the student the benefit of the doubt and a "tie will go to the runner." In other words, if I'm not certain about the persuasiveness of a presentation I will err on the side of protecting the student's right to a formal education.

Along these same lines, if the administration has a platform or a policy that they implement regarding expulsions (or when not to expel) I am happy to go along with it as long as the proposal is least restrictive as far as the student's educational rights are concerned.

I encourage agreements among the parties. It is always better when groups of people can be on the same page when discussing the best interest of a child and her education. Some hearing officers do not trust agreements. My personal position is that family members know what is best for their child and administration knows what is best for their school system and the student body.

I also feel that a student who earns it should be given every break possible when he does something stupid that results in an expulsion proceeding. That is not to say that the student is stupid but, all kids do stupid things. If he has saved his currency by doing good and acting responsibly throughout his educational career, the student should be allowed to withdraw from the piggy bank if he messes up.

Finally, an expulsion hearing, by its very nature is a punitive process. The result of hearings, however, need not always be. On several occasions I have asked parents what I can do to help them to help their child. I do anything within my jurisdiction to impose conditions in my orders that are aimed at assisting the student to get past the circumstances of the expulsion and move on with his education in a manner that suits his needs on an individual basis.

I once conducted a hearing, one of the longest I've ever done, wherein an honors student was accused of pulling a fire alarm. This is clearly an expellable offense. However, the video that the administration presented did not conclusively show the young lady pulling the fire alarm. Another video showed students laughing and pointing in the direction of the fire alarm and it was proffered that these students were part of a prank involving the fire alarm and the fire alarm puller.

The young lady accused was not only an honor student. She had an almost perfect attendance record, had no history of disciplinary issues whatsoever. She served on the student government and was chosen by the administration to escort new students throughout the building so they get acclimated and feel welcome there. Her parents were immigrants who tearfully plead the case for their daughter and impressed me with their values, particularly around issues of education.

The fire department testified that the young lady was forthright with her explanation as to how the fire alarm went off. She did not deny that she was near the alarm and was cooperative throughout the investigation. By all accounts she was consistent and credible.

I could not find by a preponderance, even based upon video evidence, that this young lady pulled the fire alarm. Likewise, based upon her unblemished record, had I found that she did pull the alarm, I do not know if I would have punished her beyond the suspension that she had served.

I did not expel.

Lately there has been a much needed and much ballyhooed movement away from the expulsion process in total. This may be good. After all, educators are there to educate and, make no mistake, kids are there and want to learn. They thrive on it.

The previous statement "this may be good" refers to the drop off in student expulsions and is made with two thoughts in mind. It is a very tough thing to imagine that a child who is struggling with the structure and socialization that school offers could possibly thrive when not allowed to go to school. Plus, there is a tremendous burden we are unwittingly placing on parents who, presumably work, and need to make arrangements for the care of an expelled child. Or not – there is a lot a kid can do to get into trouble when they are home all day with little to no supervision.

But politics being what it is and money being the master of all politics, federal and state pressures from the very top are increasingly weary of the state of American education and the apparent or *de facto* concept of removing a child from school at all. I daresay that money plays a role in this as it is quite expensive to expel a student both in the process and the after programming.

However, there are many, many situations wherein the entire milieu of a school setting is disrupted by one or more students. Educators are quite limited in resources, knowledge and ability to handle children with varying degrees of specialized needs. The demands on teachers to stick to a highly regimented curriculum and to teach to the demands of federal "suggestions" pose challenges that are compounded by even the easiest problem behaviors.

It is a very careful balancing act that administrators must undertake when making the decision to expel.

Then there are laws that REQUIRE expulsion proceedings. In certain circumstances the administration is required to bring an action for the expulsion of a student who commits certain acts. For instance, if a student brings a weapon to school Federal Law requires that the administration hold a hearing to determine whether or not she should be expelled. Sounds simple enough. However, some administrations are taking it upon themselves to determine if and when they will or will not bring an expulsion action. This cannot be. Here is the law in Connecticut which echoes the Federal Gun Free Schools Act

> Expulsion **proceedings** are required under c.g.s. 10-233d (2), section (a) if, on school grounds or at a school sponsored activity, the student was in possession of a firearm, or deadly weapon, dangerous instrument or martial arts weapon as defined 53a-3—and section (b), off school grounds, if the student did possess such a firearm in violation of section 29-3 5 or did possess and use such a firearm, instrument or weapon in the commission of a crime under chapter 952.

> Expulsion proceedings are required under c.g.s. 10-233d (2), section (C) on or off school grounds, if the student offered for sale or distribution a controlled substance, as defined in subdivision (9) of section 21 a-240, whose manufacture, distribution, sale, prescription, dispensing, transporting or possessing with intent to sell or dispense, offering, or administering is subject to criminal penalties under sections 21a-277 or 21a-278.

Let's examine this from the administration's perspective to determine exactly why they may be making this seemingly silly determination. First, it costs money to hold a hearing. Typically, they will hire an attorney to represent them, a hearing officer to preside over the proceedings, a court reporter to record the proceedings and someone on their staff needs to take the time to put together the requisite notices, exhibits and all things pertinent to the process. I would estimate that a typical hearing costs the administration somewhere in the neighborhood of $2000. This does not calculate the amount of man hours that are needed for witnesses such as school officials, teachers, security guards or police to come to the hearing. A large school system doing hundreds of "mandatory" expulsions each year can spend hundreds of thousands of dollars on the process.

I already mentioned the idea of keeping students in school as a first priority. I also acknowledge the value of structuring a student's day and "keeping them off the street" so they are less inclined to get into more trouble. But the cynical side of me keeps going back to the pressures of politics and dollars as the only conceivable reason to disobey the law and forego a "mandatory" expulsion hearing.

Our education system is under constant scrutiny. It is never good enough. It is in a perpetual state of flux as we dream up new ways to teach people how to read, write and count to ten. Whether they will acknowledge it or not politicians force our educators to "teach to the test" which is an issue for another book and another day. Likewise, behavioral issues are under the microscope and districts are, therefore leery of showing their warts. One thing that is missed is the socio-economic aspect of certain school systems, racial makeup, cultural tendency and, above all, the sheer size of the school system.

But I digress. What is happening now is that local politicians are in fear of the scrutiny and the threat of budget cuts. So they have come to the conclusion that it is better, and easier, for them not to expel students. In fact, some are not even holding MANDATORY expulsion hearings!

As I already indicated, this is against the law. As if that is not enough, it is dangerous. I would also caution administrators that, if I were a parent and my son or daughter were hurt in school I would be very upset. If I learned later that the kid that hurt my son or daughter had, previously had a weapon in school for which he escaped expulsion I would be running to my lawyer's office and the result assuredly would be costlier to the school system than a couple of hundred thousand dollars!

More on "mandatory" expulsions later. And I will end my political rantings here.

NOTES

CONCEPTS

The expulsion process is set up lawfully in quite a simple manor. It is an administrative hearing. This means that rules of evidence are relaxed and I as a hearing officer can format the hearing in the manner I deem to fit the situation.

In most situations I am required to get the answer to three related questions:

First: Did the student commit an expellable offensive? This is the foundation for it all. If the answer here is "no," I do not wish to hear any more and I will stop the hearing.

Next: If the student did commit an offense for which he or she may be expelled, should they be?

Finally: If they should be expelled, how long should that expulsion be?

There are variables in each of these that I will discuss later. Also note, inquiry in the last two questions may be based on the same factual and anecdotal information provided during the hearing.

In every case I encourage the parties to talk. I always encourage folks, in any sort of dispute to find mutual ground and reach agreement where possible. This is not to say that parties need to agree on ALL issues at hand. But, where possible, it is nicer to reach a consensus amicably (albeit regretfully/reluctantly) than it is to be told what one's fate will be.

Preliminary

For purposes of this manual I am going to assume that the administration has gone through the appropriate channels that lead us to the point of expulsion. This is to say that there was a disciplinary issue that was addressed. The student was advised of the actions that the administration had available to it and which action they were likely to pursue. I assume that the student was suspended for no more than ten days (by law) and that the hearing was scheduled in a timely fashion. (If a student is suspended and the hearing is not conducted within ten days, the student must be returned to school until a hearing is held.) I also assume that the student has been given the opportunity to receive school work during the time they are not present at school and I get upset when this is not the case.

> Due process says that one cannot be punished without having the chance to tell her side of the story.

There is also a confusing concept called "due process" which has been bent and distorted by administrators to the point that I think it is worth a brief discussion.

Due process is a concept. It is not a thing or an event. Due process is conducted in many fashions with many elements and is a conceptual part of basic human rights in our country. Due process says that one cannot be punished without having the chance to tell her side of the story. It really can be that simple.

In the world of the expulsion proceeding the question of due process is Macro (big picture) and not Micro as many administrators would have it. When we give student notice of the possibility to be suspended or expelled, we are providing them with part of their due process. When we ask a student to respond to allegations it is part of due process. When administration compiles evidence and investigates allegations, the actions are part of due process. When a student asks for character witnesses it is part of due process. Finally, the expulsion hearing itself is a piece of due process.

Due process is not simply meeting with a student and asking her what happened. This is a misnomer that is prevalent among administrators. Further, the issue as to whether or not a student was afforded due process is one to be determined by the finder of fact. It is not a piece of evidence to be offered as part of a hearing or testimony.

This is not as confusing as it sounds. It is not appropriate for an administrator to testify that he gave the student her due process. What he typically means here is that he gave the student the opportunity to respond to the allegations. Again, this is only a part of THE due process. It is not A due process.

Notice

When the determination is made to move forward with an actual expulsion proceeding, the administration must give notice of this decision to the student and/or his parent/guardian. This notice must indicate the date, time and location of the hearing and it must give the student five days "heads up" to prepare for the hearing. Therefore, the hearing should also include information about the right to and availability of legal representation for the student.

The notice must also include the allegations made against the student. In other words, exactly what is the reason or reasons that the administration has determined it should move ahead and expel the student. I personally have faith in educators that this decision is not arrived at simply or with a cavalier attitude toward any child.

The stated reason for the expulsion is important and I hold the administration to their allegations strictly. This has to be the case in the interest of fairness. A student and/or his representative cannot be expected to come to a hearing prepared to respond to allegations that are not contained in the notice of hearing. It is therefore, of the utmost importance that, in preparing the notice, the administration words its allegations carefully and precisely. On the other end of the spectrum I am quite weary of allegations that are overly broad. Being overly inclusive is as unfair as lack of specificity and I will not permit it.

The last thing to touch on here is the idea of the delivery of the notice to the student. I indicated that the letter should be sent five days prior to the scheduled hearing. This opens the door for a lot of confusion, debate and argument.

When is the "first" day of the five? Do we include weekends when we count the days? Does the hearing date count as a day? What if the student doesn't get the notice?

Without a great deal of clarity available in our education laws on the topic I will give you my interpretation.

I am going to send my notice out on Monday. Therefore, the earliest date I can have a hearing would be the following Monday. Here I count Monday, the day of mailing, through Friday. This is five days. Saturday and Sunday do not count. There is nothing to say I cannot schedule the hearing for the following Tuesday. The point is to be fair to the student and afford her the ability to respond to the allegations. The hearing should take place in a timely manner but need not be on the fifth day.

Again, if the student suspension runs its maximum ten days, the student MUST be allowed back into school unless an alternate agreement is made, regardless of when the expulsion hearing is set.

Saturdays and Sundays do not count for the purposes of our calculation. Nor do Holidays.

> The "mail box rule" leaves a lot of room for error.

The "mail box rule" is a legal concept that contends that the notice is sent to the student on the day that it was put in the public mail. This "rule" leaves a lot of room for error. For instance, the date of letter may indicate that it was written on April 3. What if April 3 was a Thursday and the mail did not go out until Tuesday because the mail process stopped for Good Friday and did not resume until the Monday after Easter? I am hard pressed to find that the notice was sent on Thursday and that it is therefore appropriate to move forward on the following Thursday, April 10.

Instead, where available, and this is rare, I look to the post mark on the envelope. If a parent is aggrieved by the lack of timely notice, I highly advise that they bring this envelope to the scheduled hearing and ask for a brief continuance of the matter until such time as they can secure appropriate representation.

Another "fail safe" in this regard is for the administration causing the notice to be delivered via certified mail. This is an added cost and adds a step to the process where the administration must track the return of the certified "green" card and produce it to show delivery of the notice. My experience is that almost invariably the green card does not come back in time or, it does not come back at all. Some people simply do not claim certified mail and I refuse to make the unilateral assumption that this is due to malevolent motives.

However, in the absence of a post marked envelope (and the absence of a student representative) the receipt for certified mail, not necessarily the claimed "green card," gives me definitive evidence of the day upon which the notice was placed in the mail.

In short, as a best practice, spend the $3 to send the notice certified. If I show up for a meeting with the administrations' attorney and a court reporter, and an issue of "notice" arises, we have wasted a lot of time and assuredly the administration will be charged the appropriate fees for the professionals in the room. This will far exceed $3.

Another fail safe is to use an independent service to make hand delivery of the hearing notice. The term "independent" is open for discussion but, I have seen and I have approved of service being made (notice delivered) by a school employee such as a security guard.

NOTES

LEGALESE

Exhibits/Hearsay/Helping Student

During the course of a hearing it is standard that the administration will want to present evidence in the customary fashion: oral and written. I will go into a bit of these here and I have enclosed a list as an appendix to some of the exhibits that are customary and helpful to me as a hearing officer. That part is easy. What is harder to explain is the things that I do not find helpful.

Let me first introduce you to another legal concept straight out of the tomes of the law school archives. "Judicial Notice" is a concept wherein a finder of fact (that's me) can admit into evidence things that are commonplace publications to the general public. For instance, newspaper articles, TV broadcasts, published books, generally accepted knowledge (in 1492 Columbus sailed the ocean blue) and I daresay, at some point, we will probably accept anything proactively placed on the Internet.

The point here is that much of what folks struggle to get "in" so I can read it and use it to base my decisions are items that I can take judicial notice of and we can skip the formalities. The best example of this is the student handbook and disciplinary policies of the Board. I am however, interested in knowing that the student was made aware of the documents and their contents.

Newspaper or other print articles are common pieces of which a hearing officer can take judicial notice. In the modern era of electronic and social media, it is very likely that items posted on line in a commonly published electronic outlet may also be thus admitted. This is an item which should scare all of us a bit.

Evidence

In an administrative hearing the rules of evidence are relaxed. The formalities of court are not strictly adhered to and some things that would not be allowed to be heard by the judge may be allowed by an administrative hearing officer. The best and most referred to example of this is "hearsay" evidence which, itself, is given an entire semester in law school.

An exhibit is just that – an exhibit. It is not "evidence" until it is admitted as a full exhibit by the hearing officer and is used or disregarded in the decision-making process. Like Due Process, evidence is a concept rather than a thing. Many exhibits and much testimony compiled together creates the evidence that is used for the final judgment. This is important because very often parties in an expulsion hearing submit a document and feel that the document itself proves or disproves allegations and that this is "evidence" refuting the contrary position.

Relaxing the rules of evidence does not mean that there are no rules and no decorum. A hearing officer has discretion about what he will allow to be presented and should be judicious in his determination of that which is relevant. This to me is the most important task of the hearing officer because, given the nature of an administrative proceeding and the lack of legal sophistication of the typical parties, this focus becomes imperative. Again, the hearing officer is there to answer narrowly defined questions as per law. It is quite easy to let exhibits and testimony lead one down many different paths that are not central to the question of expulsion as discussed earlier.

Hearsay

Hearsay is a big problem in civil and criminal courts and in administrative hearings. We spend months talking about hearsay in Law School and every lay person in the land will give you a different answer as to its definition. Be assured there is a legal definition of hearsay and some lawyers even know what it is! Some judges even know what it is. The tricky part is that lawyers and judges and hearing officers do not agree on what hearsay is and therefore, it becomes quite subjective based upon the person sitting behind the bench.

Hearsay is allowed in administrative hearings. But, a hearing officer must draw the line somewhere. Very often facts are given anecdotally, stories are told and re-told, rumors are presented for consideration and gossip is raised as a viable issue. The hearing officer has the very important job of deciding the ultimate question when it comes to allowing hearsay: which of these stories, what rumors and what gossip is probative to the central issue at hand. In other words, what do I really need to know and what is going to get me there?" This concept is called balancing "probative" against "prejudicial." The administrative hearing officer has the luxury of allowing evidence, even if it is technically hearsay, if it is something that is probative and helpful to his analysis of the matter.

> Hearsay is allowed in administrative hearings. But, a hearing officer must draw the line somewhere.

People get carried away with hearsay testimony. It is natural and is part of our everyday style of communication. "Did you hear what Joe told Emily?" "My sister told me that Sam said that Sheila is pregnant." Double and triple hearsay should not be allowed.

Under the rules of evidence there are a litany of "exceptions." These exceptions are what make a thorough understanding of the concept difficult. When you are learning facts they are taken as affirmative. When you learn about exceptions to the facts, you are learning about affirmative things that negate the original affirmative principle and it is easy to get lost in the quagmire. Get it?

The simplest "exception" to hearsay is an admission by a "party defendant." When a bad guy says he robbed a bank, testimony of the fact that he said that is not hearsay.

Another exception that is useful in an administrative expulsion hearing is the customary and standard principle. Under this concept, activity that is consistently used and accepted as policy, procedure and protocol in any given genre or industry may be considered an exception to the hearsay rules.

In an expulsion hearing, gathering student records, statements of staff, personnel and other students, publicized documents, emails, Facebook messages, Instagram pictures and the like are a customary and standard process to an investigation by administration. So, as a hearing officer I allow the investigator to testify to her findings.

Under the business records exception to the hearsay rule, the investigation and items discovered therein are also admissible. This "business record," therefore, can be testified to by, not only the investigator, but also by a supervising administrator or even a person charged with keeping the records. The witness need not have personal knowledge of the facts alleged, they just need to know that the facts were gathered in the normal course of business and compiled as a "business record" for them to be admissible.

Police Reports

There are as many rules about disclosure of police reports as there are police stations. It seems that, despite what the technicality of the law may be, each precinct feels like its own fiefdom and the rules of one may not necessarily be adhered to in another. This is very common in the release of police reports pertaining to students, usually minors, involved in criminal activity that may lead to an expulsion.

> The law is clear that, for purposes of student discipline, police reports are not deemed confidential

The law is clear that, for purposes of student discipline, police reports are not deemed confidential and can be disclosed to the administration and hence to a hearing officer. In fact, under certain circumstances authorities are required by law, to notify school officials of criminal actions perpetrated by students. This is all good in theory.

I work in one jurisdiction where I look out the window and watch the comings and goings at the police station. Moments later, in a hearing, I am told that the officer is not available or that the records from the police department were not made available to the administration.

Often the police argue that they cannot disclose information pertaining to a minor or they will not release information in an ongoing investigation. They should, but they do not and it creates problems for administrators and decision makers to say nothing of the issues that arise when detectives and officers do not show up for a hearing (often despite a subpoena to the contrary).

NOTES

3

CONSIDERATIONS

Special Education and 504 Accommodations

Prior to moving forward with an expulsion there must be a "manifestation PPT" held for any student who is identified as having and Individual Education Plan (IEP) or is receiving 504 accommodations from the school. The purpose of this hearing is to review the allegations and make a determination as to whether or not the alleged behavior is a "manifestation" of a students specialized needs or of issues relating to her 504 plan.

The PPT should be noticed and, as always, a student representative should be present. Essentially, the team is not assembled to question the veracity of the allegations. Instead, the question is this: "If the allegations are true, is it likely that the student committed the alleged violation DUE to her *identified* specialized needs?" Only if the answer to this query is "no," can the administration move forward with a plan to expel.

A manifestation PPT is not a pleasant exercise. The family of the student is often upset and will vehemently argue that the allegations are false. Likewise, they will frequently use this meeting as a time to air grievances about the implementation of the IEP and to raise questions about the true nature of the students' specialized needs. Competence will be challenged; accusations will be made. The meetings are long and tense. But, the veracity of the claim is not the core issue here. The parties must be redirected to a focus of the question of "manifestation" as opposed to a review of the established IEP or identified specialized needs.

Further, the manifestation PPT is not the time to question previously identified needs. Nor is it a time to raise new issues that attempt to explain the alleged behaviors.

All parties need to be sensitive to the emotions that, naturally, run high at this stage. In my experience, teachers, social workers and counselors are the most sensitive professionals when it comes to criticism. This is borne out of their natural propensity to want to help others and to give of themselves for another's betterment. School personnel should expect to be called out for perceived inaccuracies or even ineptitude – it is going to happen.

At the time an expulsion hearing is convened, the hearing officer should be provided with a copy of the manifestation PPT write-up containing the date and time of the meeting. It is most important to me that 1) a hearing took place and 2) the alleged actions were NOT a manifestation of specialized needs. If the findings of the manifestation PPT are that the alleged actions ARE a "manifestation" of identified, special needs, the student cannot be expelled for those alleged actions.

> **No PPT = No expulsion hearing.**

It is only after acknowledging that the PPT took place that the hearing officer even has jurisdiction to conduct an expulsion hearing. In other words, "No PPT = No expulsion hearing." The findings of the team must not be affirmative. This means that a "yes" answer to the PPT question also means that there will be no expulsion hearing.

Finally, the expulsion hearing is NOT the place to review the manifestation PPT or its findings. It is also not the place to discuss, question or review the students' special needs and should not be entertained. The hearing officer does not have jurisdiction to make findings of any kind regarding special needs or 504 accommodations.

An awkward discussion often arises when the parent or student advocate alleges that the expulsion hearing cannot take place due to the fact that the student did not get notice of and did not attend the manifestation PPT. While I am sympathetic to this argument I feel that I must assume that the jurisdictional issues and the notice issues relative to the PPT were discussed at the PPT if it were to take place at all. Therefore, based upon the fact that the meeting was held, I am not in the position to determine the legality of it having taken place much as I am not in a position to question the findings or the underlying special needs.

There are further issues to discuss when it comes to the provision of alternative educational opportunity for students with specialized needs or receiving 504 accommodations at school. Quickly then, after an expulsion hearing is conducted and it is determined that the student should be expelled, the administration must hold yet another PPT to determine the format of an appropriate alternative educational opportunity to be offered. If they disagree with me on this point I will simply make the order read that such a meeting will be convened in order to determine the appropriate alternative educational setting for a student. I feel strongly about this because during the hearing the administration is often given new information about the student that may be pertinent to his or her Individual Educational Plan and it should be brought back to the Planning and Placement team.

Request for Continuance

When a party needs more time to prepare properly for a hearing, I tend to grant a continuance for these purposes. There are two reasons for this 1) we are talking about a child's education and it should not be minimized, 2) a true "due process" argument may have merit if a student is not given the appropriate time to "prepare."(see above)

Naturally, I want to schedule the hearing as soon as possible in light of the circumstances. In this regard I always take into consideration the inconvenience/convenience of the non-moving party (the party that is not asking for the continuance; typically, the administration), the age of the student, the allegations in the notice of hearing and the remaining duration of the suspension.

In the event a party is requesting that a hearing be postponed beyond the date in which the student is supposed to return to school, I often grant the request with the following caveat: the student agrees to remain out of school until such time as the matter can be heard AND the administration will continue (I assume they already have begun) to provide the student with school work to stay current in, at least, her core academic courses.

Note: laws established in 2016 specifically recognize the validity of a request for a continuance and contemplate that a week is not an excessive amount of time to allow a student to prepare for a hearing.

NOTES

NOTES

4

THE HEARING

So let's get down to it. What does an expulsion hearing look like, what is the process and format? As mentioned earlier, an expulsion hearing is an administrative hearing. As a hearing officer, I sit as the "judge," arbiter and referee of the process. I also have leeway as to the manner in which I wish to conduct the hearing. There are statutes and rules that guide administrative hearings but, in general, they should follow the typical decorum of a formal court room. Each side will be afforded the ability to present their position and the other side will be afforded the opportunity to respond. Evidence will be presented and cross-examined. The same courtesy afforded in a meeting, a dinner table or a court of law will apply here.

An administrative hearing officer must be seen as approachable. He is there as a guide to the process and, very often, will hold the hand of one or both parties in order to walk them through it. This is not to say that a hearing officer should be, or is, bias. Instead, the hearing officer has the duty to try to even the playing field for a less sophisticated or disadvantaged party. I feel strongly about this. Particularly where education of a child is at stake.

In this same "spirit," I support preliminary discussions among the parties to come to a resolution of matters on their own. As mentioned earlier, it is always better for both sides to give a little for the benefit of the student and to reach an agreement that is satisfactory to both. Otherwise, I will make an order and one party will feel that it was unfair or that they "lost" which invariably leaves them unhappy and dissatisfied with the process.

My one request, however, is that *preliminary* discussions take place preliminarily. It is awkward, unfair and somewhat disrespectful to ask witnesses and other folks to sit idle for lengthy periods of time while the parties to a dispute begin settlement discussions behind closed doors. I have sat for two hours awaiting the outcome of such conversations only to be told that the hearing would not move forward. This does not make me happy.

Recording

All hearings must be recorded. It is the responsibility of the administration to arrange for a recording service to be present to make this happen. Admittedly, the statutes pertaining to the recording is ambiguous as to how it should be conducted. Some jurisdictions, in an effort to save money, have begun to opt to record the proceedings themselves. I am not a big fan of this at all.

> It is the responsibility of the administration to arrange for a recording service ...

There are a few different manners of recording the proceedings I have seen. First, some jurisdictions have invested in technology to make an electronic recording of administrative hearings. This is commendable. However, even professional recording companies have not completely gone away from "analog" recordings as they are still not confident in the reliability of hardware available to make digital recordings. One concern is that there is not a readily available manner in which to monitor the progress of the recording as it is taking place. So, if the hearing is conducted and the machine breaks in the middle of it, the entire proceeding may need to be re-heard.

Next, there are jurisdictions that are still using cassette recorders in proceedings. Other than the age of the equipment and the same reliability as mentioned with digital recordings the main issue I have with cassette recordings is the manner in which they are stored. More on this next.

Finally, I have been to several hearings where the attorney for the administration records the proceedings on her phone or tablet. I cannot stress enough that this is the least preferred manner in documenting a hearing.

The overarching principle behind recording any and all proceedings must be the preservation of the recording for future use. A vital component of the recording is the "chain of custody" of the recorded materials. So, when a cassette recording is haphazardly stored along with a file in a cabinet somewhere the chances of it getting lost are heightened. My concern over the attorney recording is that, not only can the recording get lost or deleted from her phone or tablet but, it just opens the door for a question of the chain of custody of the recording.

This is not to suggest that an administration will go out of its way to erase or lose a recording. I am not a conspiracy theorist who believes that anyone would intentionally delete or alter some or all of a recording to promote their interest. However, it just seems to me that we should remove any and all opportunities for any claims of impropriety.

I have presided over matters where a stenographer has captured the proceedings. This is a dying art. This is the preferred method obviously, but, I can imagine it must be very expensive.

Basic Principles of Law

Before a hearing begins I read a statement into the record. It is a bit long but it lays forth the legal concepts and requirements pertaining to the entire proceeding. Here it is:

> I will now call to order a special meeting of the impartial hearing board of the _____ **Board of Education** which was called for the purpose of conducting a student expulsion hearing.
>
> The time is _____ on _____.
>
> I am Attorney Michael Mackniak, the designated impartial hearing officer of the _____ **Board of Education**.
>
> It is the intention of the impartial hearing board to conduct The hearing in executive session, pursuant to the freedom of Information act, specifically c.g.s. 1-200(6)(e) and 1-210 (b)(11) and (17), as the names of the students involved, their educational

records and personally identifiable information contained in Those records are likely to be discussed. This board will now Move into executive session for the purpose of conducting the Hearing, with the following persons invited to present testimony or opinion or to represent the various parties to the Proceedings:

Attorney for the administration:
_____

Assistant/superintendent of schools:
_____

Principal/asst. principal:
_____

Name of school:
_____

Teacher:
_____

School officer (detective):
_____

_____ police department

The student who is the subject of this expulsion hearing:
_____

The parents /guardian of the student who is the subject of the expulsion proceeding.
_____

Attorney – for the student:
_____

THE HEARING

Court reporter:
_____

We are now in executive session. The time is _____.

The doors to the hearing room are closed.

Pursuant to section 10-233d of the Connecticut general Statutes, the public _____ **School Administration** has initiated this action regarding the expulsion of _____. The student is a/an _____ grader at _____ school. His/Her date of birth is _____ and he/she is _____ years of age. This student IS/IS NOT a special education student. A PPT hearing WAS/WAS NOT conducted, where it was determined that the student's conduct WAS/ WAS NOT a manifestation of his/her disability.

Pursuant to section 10-233d the impartial hearing board is required to conduct a hearing in accordance with the Uniform Administrative Procedure Act, Section 4-176e through 4-180a inclusive and 4-181a:

If the student is expelled and is **under the age of 16**, (s)he must **be** offered an alternate educational program.

Any pupil expelled for the first time who is **between the ages of sixteen and eighteen** and who wishes to continue his education shall be offered an alternative educational opportunity if he complies with conditions established by his local board of education.

In the case of a student between the ages of sixteen and eighteen who is excluded because of conduct involving a firearm, deadly weapon, deadly instrument, martial arts weapon, or the sale or distribution of controlled substances on school grounds or at a school sponsored activity, or for a student who has been expelled previously, the board of education is not obligated under law to provide an alternative educational opportunity.

Expulsion proceedings are required under c.g.s. 10-233d (2), section (a) if, on school grounds or at a school sponsored activity, the student was in possession of a firearm, or deadly weapon, dangerous instrument or martial arts weapon as defined 53a-3 – and section (b), off school grounds, if the student did possess such a firearm in violation of section 29-3 5 or did possess and use such a firearm, instrument or weapon in the commission of a crime under chapter 952.

Expulsion proceedings are required under c.g.s. 10-233d (2), section (C) on or off school grounds, if the student offered for sale or distribution a controlled substance, as defined in subdivision (9) of section 21 a-240, whose manufacture, distribution, sale, prescription, dispensing, transporting or possessing with intent to sell or dispense, offering, or administering is subject to criminal penalties under sections 21a-277 or 21a-278.

Pursuant to cgs 10-233d the _____ **school administration** has alleged that the conduct of the student violated publicized policies of the board of education or posed a danger to himself/herself and others and/or caused a serious disruption to the educational process.

The purpose of this hearing is to gain as many facts as possible in order to render a determination of whether the student in question committed prohibited conduct. The burden of proof is on the _____ **Administration** to prove by a preponderance of the evidence that the student committed prohibited conduct.

All officially interested persons will be given an opportunity to make a presentation. We shall hear first from the administration. Thereafter, the student will be provided an opportunity to respond to the school's presentation.

I will now ask anyone who expects to speak, to stand, and take the oath or affirmation. Please raise your right hand.

Do you solemnly swear that the evidence you are to present concerning the case in question shall be the truth, the whole truth, and nothing but the truth, so help you God?

This statement goes a long way to the interpretation of the laws and is concise albeit a bit heavy on the "legal mumbo jumbo." So, for the next section of this manual I will break it down, not necessarily in order, into its component parts.

I want to point out a couple of quagmires of the language that I have had struggles with over the years.

Mandatory Expulsion Hearings

Earlier I mentioned the issue about when an administration MUST bring forth an Expulsion **HEARING**. In Connecticut, as is mentioned in my opening statement, the law is set forth at CGS Section 10-233d (a-c). The law says that if a student has possession of a weapon etc. on school grounds the school must move to expel him. Likewise, if the student uses a weapon, in school or out of school in the commission of a crime, the school must move to expel. It is interesting to note here that the mere possession of the weapon is a crime so the student is "possessing and committing" at the same time.

> **The mere possession of the weapon is a crime so the student is "possessing and committing" at the same time.**

In either case, the law is based on the federal law called the Gun Free Schools Act. The federal law recommends that, in the case of possession of a weapon on school grounds or in the commission of a crime on or off school grounds, the student should be expelled for up to a year.

The law then goes on to state that the Hearing officer in either case has the discretion to amended this recommendation on a case by case basis. Thank you very much.

I point this out because it is a common misconception that a "mandatory hearing" means that a student MUST be expelled and that the expulsion MUST be for a year.

Finally, with regard to the rules about possession of drugs or alcohol on school grounds or at a school sponsored activity, the law technically states that an expulsion hearing is mandatory if the student was in possession AND was dispensing the substance. This can easily be interpreted to say that it is necessary to actually "catch the student in the act" of distributing in order to give rise to a mandatory expulsion hearing.

Further references in the language lead us to other statutes which define "distribution." The short answer is that, if a student has enough of an illegal substance in her possession while on school grounds or at a school sponsored activity, to statutorily be deemed "in possession with intent to distribute or sell," the language pertaining to a mandatory expulsion hearing will apply.

If the student is not in possession of such amounts, there is nothing to say that the administration should not bring an action for expulsion based upon the student's mere possession of the substance.

Expulsion for Off Campus Activity

Yes, a student can be expelled for activity which occurs off of school grounds. I mentioned the use of weapons in the commission of a crime above.

Note that the school bus, bus stop, playground, football field, bleachers, roof, another school all are considered school grounds for these purposes.

Whenever there is a nexus between the activity, the location and the home school, the student is deemed to be on school grounds. The same analysis should apply for "school sponsored activities" such as away games, dances, graduation ceremonies etc. Again, improper use of the Internet where it involves the school, administration and other students is increasingly prevalent and may result in expulsion from school.

As previously mentioned the police are required to inform the school of the arrest of students under certain circumstances. This may or may not give rise to an expulsion.

Expulsions for activity off of school grounds are the most problematic of all disciplinary matters and I will detail here the reasons.

In an expulsion hearing for activity that occurred on school grounds or at a school sponsored activity the school must show by a preponderance of the evidence that the alleged activity violated publicized policy of the Board of Education, **OR** endangers the student or others, (Staff included) **OR** "**seriously**" disrupts the educational process. The key words here are highlighted. Administrators do not need to prove all of the above. In most circumstances violation of one of the three is enough to get me over the threshold as to whether or not an expellable offense did occur. Administrators often get confused here and fall all over themselves to prove that the alleged actions of the student violate all three of these elements. It is not necessary and becomes cumbersome.

Where an off campus activity is involved, the inquiry changes. Here the administration must show by a preponderance of the evidence that the alleged activity 1) violated publicized policy of the Board of Education, **AND** "**seriously**" disrupts the educational process.

As for the first element here, see my notes on "judicial notice" above. Testimony that the policies of the board of education were publicized and provided to the student will usually suffice to meet this first burden. The second element is tricky and I take it quite seriously.

We are given some guidance as to how to define disruptive of the educational process. (Whether it is "seriously" disruptive is a matter of subjectivity I suppose.) For instance, proximity to a school and the involvement of other students is one identified barometer as is the likely presence of gang related activity. Interestingly, the law allows us to consider the involvement of alcohol in this determination but does not make a reference to other drugs. (In my analysis I do consider the presence of all substance during the alleged violation.)

Administrators often attempt to testify that their investigation into an off campus activity took them away from their regular duties at school and therefore are disruptive of the educational process. I do NOT subscribe to this argument.

Executive Session

An expulsion hearing is a public hearing. It is an administrative hearing that is conducted by the board of education. Statute provides that a Board of education can designate members of its board to hear the matter, the full board to hear the matter, or, an independent third party to act in its place in this regard. It is confusing but, a hearing officer, like myself is referred to and refers to themselves as a "hearing board" even if there is one of them.

> A hearing officer is referred to as a "hearing board" even if there is only one of them.

Freedom of Information applies to a Board of Education. However, public interest in protecting confidentiality and privacy of matters pertaining to minor children outweighs the public's interest in participating in the process. So, an expulsion hearing is set up in two ways.

First the notice is sent and a hearing is convened "in public session." This means that, presumably, anyone from the public is invited into the room and can hear the me read into the record the first three or four paragraphs of the Opening Statement. I have presided over thousands of hearings and have never once had anyone other than interested parties show up to get their "dirty laundry" fix regarding student expulsions.

Then, as per the Opening Statement, I advise the parties that we will move into "executive session" for the remainder of the hearing. It is at this point, depending upon who is in the room and the level of animosity between the parties that I may, or may not ask witnesses to step outside so as not to be tainted by evidence presented before they are to testify.

Typically, however, I note that the hearing room doors are closed (after I make sure that they are) and I then proceed in what I have created as a "private" proceeding. This is "executive session" for purposes of an expulsion hearing.

Bifurcated Hearing

In addition to the "fictitious" creation of an "executive session," many jurisdictions like to concoct fictitious segregation of issues for an expulsion hearing. As noted above and discussed in detail earlier, there are three major issues before me in any Expulsion hearing: Did the student commit an expellable offense AND should she be expelled? If so how long/what should be the duration of the expulsion?

It is helpful to bifurcate the proceedings along these lines so that all parties have a clear understanding of the specific issue to be discussed at a specific time. Some hearing officers will, quite literally, ask all parties to leave the room while they ponder the issue *"Did the student commit an expellable offense?"* And ask them to return after he has made his decision.

Then, he will reconvene the matter and conduct inquiry into the second phase of the hearing focusing on *Should the student be expelled?* Personally, I think this is overkill, and I do not practice such ceremony in my hearings.

There is a great deal of evidence that is pertinent to the totality of the circumstances which may be rendered prejudicial or irrelevant to one part of the hearing or another if we strictly bifurcate along these lines. A good hearing officer must be able to hear the evidence as it is presented and distinguish which pieces are probative versus prejudicial. Any trier of fact has to be given the benefit of the doubt that he/she has the ability to do this and, if not, the parties are welcome to raise objections to discuss the matter as it comes up.

This is not to say that I do not see merit in the practice of bifurcating the matter. I have asked parties in the past to stipulate to facts that they could agree upon so that we do not need to belabor them formally. This is a slippery slope, because sometimes more information is better and, in theory, stipulated facts need not be picked apart or explained to flesh out the "evidence" that they present. One party may feel, rightfully, that if they are not allowed to present the evidence they have to prove a stipulated fact, they may be prejudiced as to another important part of the hearing altogether.

If this is the case, they should not stipulate.

NOTES

NOTES

SELF REPRESENTED PARTIES

Presenting the Case

The burden of proof in any expulsion proceeding is on the administration who must prove "by a preponderance of the evidence" that the conduct of the student was an expellable offense. This is not a criminal trial and I am careful not to allow either party to treat it as such. First, the standard of proof burden is not the same (Beyond a reasonable doubt in criminal matters). A preponderance standard dictates that I have to be able to say that it is "more likely than not" that the activity alleged did occur.

Therefore, the administration is asked to present its case first. As is noted above, after the Administration presents its case, the student will have the opportunity to respond. The parties will examine and cross examine witnesses and evidence presented. Then the student will have the opportunity to present her case. The same procedure will follow until both sides have finished or "rest."

Very often the parties come to the hearing with many witnesses and documents that they would like me to hear in order to make my decision as to pertinent issues during a hearing. This is fine and the "rules of evidence" are supposed to be relaxed in an administrative hearing. This does not mean that there are no rules.

As previously mentioned, the administrator or designee who conducted the investigation into the matter is the person who is in the best position to speak to his/her findings AND the documents they have included as evidence. Likewise, a character witness who prepares a document pertaining to the good nature of the student is in the best position to testify to her beliefs if she is present. When a witness is present to testify to a document she prepared, she should be allowed to testify to it. This is the "best evidence" rule and it is weightier than all other such evidence.

Police officers should present testimony about their investigations. Despite case law and statute to the contrary, MANY police departments contend that they cannot provide reports or notes about an ongoing criminal investigation AND that the confidential aspect of pertaining to children's matters precludes them from providing evidence in any form for an expulsion hearing. Nothing can be further from the truth but, the arguments persist as does the standoff between school administrations and local police policy.

In these matters, the hearing officer must be creative and sympathetic to the roadblock that these erroneous policies may present and rule accordingly. As mentioned earlier, I believe that a police report can be admitted under hearsay exceptions where it is standard practice for an administrator to gather the report from the police department even if an officer is not there to testify to it. Where there is no report and no officer, the administration must rely upon its internal investigation to prove the allegations set forth in the hearing.

Witness Testimony

During the presentation of its case, the designee of either side tend to try to present the same testimony by several different witnesses. I do not subscribe to this practice. When a witness is presenting testimony about an event that he was involved in or saw firsthand, I do not need to hear a second or third witness testify to the exact same course of events. I do not think it is MORE probative because I have three people reciting the same facts over to me. In fact, it often feels like piling on and, in most cases, is overkill. I do like testimony that adds or supplements information already in evidence to the extent that it is probative.

A common trap that parties fall into when they are presenting a case without representation by a lawyer, is that they tend to testify for their witness. As previously mentioned, I will assist an administrator who is self-represented (pro se) just as much as I would assist a pro se student/family. But, I cannot allow an administrator to present evidence by testifying for his witness.

A common mistake made in this regard is as follows: "Teacher, please look behind exhibit 3. This is a copy of the statement given by janitor on February 3."

STOP!! Do you see what the administrator is doing here? He is not only leading his witness. He is, in fact testifying. It is the job of the witness to identify and describe exhibit 3. The administrator elicits the information via questions designed to paint a picture for the hearing officer as to the point he is trying to make.

Another common mistake is for witnesses to testify affirmatively as to questions of fact. I have mentioned this earlier and I think it is worth mentioning again. It is very rare that a student alleges that she was not given the opportunity to tell the administrations her side of the story. Still, administrators go out of their way to let me know that they allowed the student to tell her side of the story. Under questioning I hear this "I met with the student in my office and gave her Due Process."

STOP!! You brought the student into your office and offered her the opportunity to tell you her side of the story. The hearing officer will determine whether or not the students Due Process rights were violated.

> Both the student and the administration should identify one person who will present the evidence to the hearing officer.

Both the student and the administration should identify one person who will present the evidence to the hearing officer. This designee will act like the lawyer in a TV courtroom drama and has the job of presenting the case of either side accordingly.

Cross Examining Student Witnesses

Very often students provide the administration with statements about the allegations giving rise to a hearing. It is natural that the responding student, the one who faces possible expulsion, would like to have the opportunity to cross examine the makers of these statements in order to call into question their veracity and the character of the student making them.

There is strong public policy about this in all aspects of American Jurisprudence. Simply put, the Due Process rights of a student who faces allegations which could lead to expulsion are outweighed by the right to privacy and other protective considerations we must provide to minor children in these proceedings.

To further illustrate this concept, all evidence in an Expulsion Hearing should be "redacted." Names and identification of students other than the responding student should be crossed out, erased or otherwise removed from all evidence set forth. Logically, if we find it important enough to erase a name from a document for privacy and protection reasons, it makes little sense that we should subject students to testifying in person in an administrative hearing.

The criminal courts have mechanisms to get around this sticky problem which are used in extreme circumstances. The persuasive argument here is that the accused stands to lose his liberty if not allowed to cross examine certain witnesses.

In an administrative hearing, the student does not have a liberty issue. Further the argument that there is a property value to an education has been debunked by the highest courts, particularly when the student can be afforded an alternative educational opportunity.

NOTES

NOTES

6

THE DECISION-MAKING PROCESS

Should the student be expelled? How long?

Assuming that we have moved through the first portion of the hearing and we have made a finding that, indeed, an expellable offense DID occur, we move to the second stage. Here we ask whether or not the student should be expelled.

Here is an analogy I use often: When we do well and are upstanding citizens, it is like we are putting coins into a piggy bank. This is our collateral. If we mess up and do something stupid or bad, it does not mean that we are stupid or bad. Therefore, we should be allowed to draw against some of our collateral.

It works for me. I use this analogy to assist in the analysis of whether or not a student should be expelled from school (and for what duration).

In this, the second part of our "bifurcated hearing" I go beyond the mere facts of the case and look more into anecdotal information about a student as a person and evidence as to their character as a citizen of the school.

Here is where I allow evidence that will give me insight into the student as a person in terms of:

> **Attendance:** do they want to be at school in the first place? Do they skip classes? Are they excessively tardy, sick or just do not go to school?
>
> **Grades:** How is their academic performance?

Disciplinary History: Is their tendency toward being a good student or a problem in the educational environment which impacts others?

I do not need a recitation of facts already in evidence. I can read the exhibits given to me in order to determine a student's GPA or disciplinary history. I will do so in a pinch. But, what I prefer is that the administration and the students' parents/guardians give me an unbiased picture of how the student is in the big picture.

It may seem surprising but, generally parents and the administration agree about the general nature of a student. The administration acknowledges the qualities that a student possesses and the parents can acknowledge where their son/daughter can do better. It is very rare that I have to cut through the evidence to make my own determination about the propensity of a student to be trouble in school or not.

This is why I appreciate a recommendation from the administration about the duration of an expulsion for each particular student. The recommendation shows me that the Administrator has truly given thought to the process and the appropriate punishment in each situation. Likewise, the student and her representatives can get a feel for the same and walk away with a broader understanding of the reasoning behind the expulsion or recommendation.

> An expulsion proceeding is a good time for both student and administration to "re-group" and figure out what is working and what is not.

The best recommendations fall in line with my philosophy that an expulsion proceeding is a good time for both student and administration to "re-group" and figure out what is working and what is not. This concept reaches to the parents/guardians of a student and may even help them to help their child. If it is within my jurisdiction I am happy to make orders for either side to implement strategies that will 1) impress upon the student the seriousness of the matter and 2) help them to take ownership of their behaviors at school and at home.

THE DECISION-MAKING PROCESS

I do not have to accept the recommendations and, sometimes, I do not. It is common that an administrator will simply recommend that the student is expelled for a full calendar year (the most allowable by law) and leave it to me, the hearing officer, to make the determination for them. In some ways this speaks volumes about the student, the administration, or both.

Note, a recommendation should not be made that the student is not allowed to return to their particular school. This is outside the purview of the hearing officer and is not an appropriate issue for an expulsion hearing.

Alternative Educational Opportunity

During the recommendation phase and final disposition of a matter, it is helpful to explore the possibility (and likelihood) that a student will be afforded an alternative educational opportunity.

As my preliminary statement reads, if a student is under sixteen, she MUST be offered an alternative educational opportunity.

A student who is between sixteen and eighteen will be offered an alternative educational opportunity if 1) they have not been expelled before and 2) they agree to comply with conditions set forth by the Board of Education (or the hearing officer). At a minimum, these conditions are that the student will participate and cooperate with the alternative education and they will not get into further trouble. Some jurisdictions want to see a student perform some community service or write a letter of apology to aggrieved individuals. I do not see harm in these conditions and I will typically order them as well as other items such as counseling or drug testing. This is where we can be creative and truly think outside the box about the manner in which we can assist a student and his family with issues that may go well beyond behavior at school.

The statement also contains language about a student who engages in activity that would give rise to a mandatory expulsion hearing. According to statute, a student (16-18 years old) expelled due to possession of a weapon or controlled substance ON school grounds, shall not be offered an alternative educational opportunity.

A student who is eighteen or older is considered an adult. All notice of pending hearings must go to the student. The student should be deemed to have the capacity to represent herself and must be in attendance at the expulsion proceeding. If the parent of the student shows without the student, the hearing should not go forward. Likewise, if the STUDENT does not receive notice of the hearing according to statute, the hearing shall not go forward.

NOTES

NOTES

7

I REST

As a final matter, I want to mention to you a philosophy I learned from my father who was an educator for thirty-three years and retired as assistant superintendent of schools. He was in charge of expulsions as part of his final position and we would have, and still do have, long discussions about school discipline. The inquiry that my father had with his staff always went first to making a determination as to whether the school had done all it could to provide a productive educational environment for each student before moving to expel.

I try to make the same inquiry within the context of an expulsion hearing over which I preside. Coming from a family of educators, I bristle and I am sensitive to allegations from student representatives about all that a school has not done or should do. "Charity starts in the home." But, as an impartial hearing officer I have become more alert to the validity of some compelling discussion in this regard and I do all I can to foster a productive dialogue and to help where I can. I think I have had a great deal of success and most people leave my hearings feeling that they were a productive part of a process and were not forced into an unfair or unreasonable disposition.

Where I can be a mediator I will be. Where I can bring levity to an uncomfortable situation, I try. Where I can be an authority figure to impress upon a student the seriousness of the matter at hand, I oblige both for the benefit of the educator and the family. Where I can remind people that we are all in one room for a common goal – the education of OUR children – I am honored and, I am grateful for the opportunity.

NOTES

APPENDIX A

Important Documents Constituting Evidence in a Student Expulsion Hearing

1. Notice of Hearing
2. Complaint
3. Statements of incident
4. Police Reports
5. Letter to parents re findings
6. Suspension notice
7. PPT paperwork
8. Code of conduct student handbook
9. Receipt of student handbook
10. Academic record
11. Disciplinary record
12. Attendance record

APPENDIX B

Sec. 10-233d. Expulsion of pupils. (a)(1) Any local or regional board of education, at a meeting at which three or more members of such board are present, or the impartial hearing board established pursuant to subsection (b) of this section, may expel, subject to the provisions of this subsection, any pupil whose conduct on school grounds or at a school-sponsored activity is violative of a publicized policy of such board or is seriously disruptive of the educational process or endangers persons or property or whose conduct off school grounds is violative of such policy and is seriously disruptive of the educational process, provided a majority of the board members sitting in the expulsion hearing vote to expel and that at least three affirmative votes for expulsion are cast. In making a determination as to whether conduct is seriously disruptive of the educational process, the board of education or impartial hearing board may consider, but such consideration shall not be limited to: (A) Whether the incident occurred within close proximity of a school; (B) whether other students from the school were involved or whether there was any gang involvement; (C) whether the conduct involved violence, threats of violence or the unlawful use of a weapon, as defined in section 29-38, and whether any injuries occurred; and (D) whether the conduct involved the use of alcohol.

(2) Expulsion proceedings pursuant to this section, except as provided in subsection (i) of this section shall be required whenever there is reason to believe that any pupil (A) on school grounds or at a school sponsored activity, was in possession of a firearm, as defined in 18 USC 921, as amended from time to time, or deadly weapon, dangerous instrument or martial arts weapon, as defined in section 53a-3, (B) off school grounds, did possess such a firearm in violation of section 29-35 or did possess and use such a firearm, instrument or weapon in the commission of a crime under chapter 952, or (C) on or off school grounds, offered for sale or distribution a controlled substance, as defined in subdivision (9) of section 21a-240, whose manufacture, distribution, sale, prescription, dispensing, transporting or possessing with intent to sell or dispense, offering, or administering is subject to criminal penalties under sections 21a-277 and 21a-278. Such a pupil shall be expelled for one calendar year if the local or regional board of education or impartial hearing board finds that the pupil did so possess or so possess and use, as appropriate, such a firearm, instrument or weapon or did so offer for sale or distribution such a controlled substance, provided the board of education or the hearing board may modify the period of expulsion for a pupil on a case by case basis.

(3) Unless an emergency exists, no pupil shall be expelled without a formal hearing held pursuant to sections 4-176e to 4-180a, inclusive, and section 4-181a, provided whenever such pupil is a minor, the notice required by section 4-177 and section 4-180 shall also be given to the parents or guardian of the pupil. If an emergency exists, such hearing shall be held as soon after the expulsion as possible.

(b) For purposes of conducting expulsion hearings as required by subsection (a) of this section, any local or regional board of education or any two or more of such boards in cooperation may establish an impartial hearing board of one or more persons. No member of any such board or boards shall be a member of the hearing board. The hearing board shall have the authority to conduct the expulsion hearing and render a final decision in accordance with the provisions of sections 4-176e to 4-180a, inclusive, and section 4-181a.

(c) In determining the length of an expulsion and the nature of the alternative educational opportunity to be offered under subsection (d), the local or regional board of education, or the impartial hearing board established pursuant to subsection (b) of this section, may receive and consider evidence of past disciplinary problems which have led to removal from a classroom, suspension or expulsion of such pupil.

(d) Notwithstanding the provisions of subsection (a) of section 10-220, local and regional boards of education shall only be required to offer an alternative educational opportunity in accordance with this section. Any pupil under sixteen years of age who is expelled shall be offered an alternative educational opportunity during the period of expulsion, provided any parent or guardian of such pupil who does not choose to have his or her child enrolled in an alternative program shall not be subject to the provisions of section 10-184. Any pupil expelled for the first time who is between the ages of sixteen and eighteen and who wishes to continue his or her education shall be offered an alternative educational opportunity if he or she complies with conditions established by his or her local or regional board of education. Such alternative may include, but shall not be limited to, the placement of a pupil who is at least sixteen years of age in an adult education program pursuant to section 10-69. A local or regional board of education shall count the expulsion of a pupil when he was under sixteen years of age for purposes of determining whether an alternative educational opportunity is required for such pupil when he is between the ages of sixteen and eighteen. A local or regional board of education may offer an alternative educational opportunity to a pupil for whom such alternative educational opportunity is not required pursuant to this section.

(e) Notwithstanding the provisions of subsection (d) of this section concerning the provision of an alternative educational opportunity for pupils between the ages of sixteen and eighteen, local and regional boards of education shall not be required to offer such alternative to any pupil between the ages of sixteen and eighteen who is expelled because of conduct which endangers persons if it is determined at the expulsion hearing that the conduct for which the pupil is expelled involved (1) possession of a firearm, as defined in 18 USC 921, as amended from time to time, or deadly weapon, dangerous instrument or martial arts weapon, as defined in section 53a-3, on school property or at a school-sponsored activity or (2) offering for sale or distribution on school property or at a school-sponsored activity a controlled substance, as defined in subdivision (9) of section 21a-240, whose manufacture, distribution, sale, prescription, dispensing, transporting or possessing with the intent to sell or dispense, offering, or administration is subject to criminal penalties under sections 21a-277 and 21a-278. If a pupil is expelled pursuant to this section for possession of a firearm or deadly weapon the board of education shall report the violation to the local police department or in the case of a student enrolled in a regional vocational-technical school to the state police. If a pupil is expelled pursuant to this section for the sale or distribution of such a controlled substance, the board of education shall refer the pupil to an appropriate state or local agency for rehabilitation, intervention or job training, or any combination thereof, and inform the agency of its action. Whenever a local or regional board of education notifies a pupil between the ages of sixteen and eighteen or the parents or guardian of such pupil that an expulsion hearing will be held, the notification shall include a statement that the board of education is not required to offer an alternative educational opportunity to any pupil who is found to have engaged in the conduct described in this subsection.

(f) Whenever a pupil is expelled pursuant to the provisions of this section, notice of the expulsion and the conduct for which the pupil was expelled shall be included on the pupil's cumulative educational record. Such notice, except for notice of an expulsion based on possession of a firearm or deadly weapon as described in subsection (a) of this section, shall be expunged from the cumulative educational record by the local or regional board of education if a pupil graduates from high school.

(g) A local or regional board of education may adopt the decision of a pupil expulsion hearing conducted by another school district provided such local or regional board of education or impartial hearing board shall hold a hearing pursuant to the provisions of subsection (a) of this section which shall be limited to a determination of whether the conduct which was the basis for the expulsion would also warrant expulsion under the policies of such board. The pupil shall be excluded from school pending such hearing. The excluded student shall be offered an alternative educational opportunity in accordance with the provisions of subsections (d) and (e) of this section.

(h) Whenever a pupil against whom an expulsion hearing is pending withdraws from school after notification of such hearing but before the hearing is completed and a decision rendered pursuant to this section, (1) notice of the pending expulsion hearing shall be included on the pupil's cumulative educational record and (2) the local or regional board of education or impartial hearing board shall complete the expulsion hearing and render a decision. If such pupil enrolls in school in another school district, such pupil shall not be excluded from school in the other district pending completion of the expulsion hearing pursuant to this subsection unless an emergency exists, provided nothing in this subsection shall limit the authority of the local or regional board of education for such district to suspend the pupil or to conduct its own expulsion hearing in accordance with this section.

(i) Prior to conducting an expulsion hearing for a child requiring special education and related services described in subparagraph (A) of subdivision (5) of section 10-76a, a planning and placement team shall convene to determine whether the misconduct was caused by the child's disability. If it is determined that the misconduct was caused by the child's disability, the child shall not be expelled. The planning and placement team shall reevaluate the child for the purpose of modifying the child's individualized education program to address the misconduct and to ensure the safety of other children and staff in the school. If it is determined that the misconduct was not caused by the child's disability, the child may be expelled in accordance with the provisions of this section applicable to children who do not require special education and related services. Notwithstanding the provisions of subsections (d) and (e) of this section, whenever a child requiring such special education and related services is expelled, an alternative educational opportunity, consistent with such child's educational needs shall be provided during the period of expulsion.

(j) An expelled pupil may apply for early readmission to school. Except as provided in this subsection, such readmission shall be at the discretion of the local or regional board of education. The board of education may delegate authority for readmission decisions to the superintendent of schools for the school district. If the board delegates such authority, readmission shall be at the discretion of the superintendent. Readmission decisions shall not be subject to appeal to Superior Court. The board or superintendent, as appropriate, may condition such readmission on specified criteria.

(k) Local and regional boards of education shall submit to the Commissioner of Education such information on expulsions for the possession of weapons as required for purposes of the Gun-Free Schools Act of 1994, 20 USC 8921 et seq., as amended from time to time.

APPENDIX B

Sec. 53a-3. Definitions. Except where different meanings are expressly specified, the following terms have the following meanings when used in this title:

(1) "Person" means a human being, and, where appropriate, a public or private corporation, a limited liability company, an unincorporated association, a partnership, a government or a governmental instrumentality;

(2) "Possess" means to have physical possession or otherwise to exercise dominion or control over tangible property;

(3) "Physical injury" means impairment of physical condition or pain;

(4) "Serious physical injury" means physical injury which creates a substantial risk of death, or which causes serious disfigurement, serious impairment of health or serious loss or impairment of the function of any bodily organ;

(5) "Deadly physical force" means physical force which can be reasonably expected to cause death or serious physical injury;

(6) "Deadly weapon" means any weapon, whether loaded or unloaded, from which a shot may be discharged, or a switchblade knife, gravity knife, billy, blackjack, bludgeon, or metal knuckles. The definition of "deadly weapon" in this subdivision shall be deemed not to apply to section 29-38 or 53-206;

(7) "Dangerous instrument" means any instrument, article or substance which, under the circumstances in which it is used or attempted or threatened to be used, is capable of causing death or serious physical injury, and includes a "vehicle" as that term is defined in this section and includes a dog that has been commanded to attack, except a dog owned by a law enforcement agency of the state or any political subdivision thereof or of the federal government when such dog is in the performance of its duties under the direct supervision, care and control of an assigned law enforcement officer;

(8) "Vehicle" means a "motor vehicle" as defined in section 14-1, a snowmobile, any aircraft, or any vessel equipped for propulsion by mechanical means or sail;

(9) "Peace officer" means a member of the Division of State Police within the Department of Public Safety or an organized local police department, a chief inspector or inspector in the Division of Criminal Justice, a state marshal while exercising authority granted under any provision of the general statutes, a judicial marshal in the performance of the duties of a judicial marshal, a conservation officer or special conservation officer, as defined in section 26-5, a constable who performs criminal law enforcement duties, a special policeman appointed under section 29-18, 29-18a or 29-19, an adult probation officer, an official of the Department of Correction authorized by the Commissioner of Correction to make arrests in a correctional institution or facility, any investigator in the investigations unit of the office of the State Treasurer or any special agent of the federal government authorized to enforce the provisions of Title 21 of the United States Code;

(10) "Firefighter" means any agent of a municipality whose duty it is to protect life and property therein as a member of a duly constituted fire department whether professional or volunteer;

(11) A person acts "intentionally" with respect to a result or to conduct described by a statute defining an offense when his conscious objective is to cause such result or to engage in such conduct;

(12) A person acts "knowingly" with respect to conduct or to a circumstance described by a statute defining an offense when he is aware that his conduct is of such nature or that such circumstance exists;

(13) A person acts "recklessly" with respect to a result or to a circumstance described by a statute defining an offense when he is aware of and consciously disregards a substantial and unjustifiable risk that such result will occur or that such circumstance exists. The risk must be of such nature and degree that disregarding it constitutes a gross deviation from the standard of conduct that a reasonable person would observe in the situation;

(14) A person acts with "criminal negligence" with respect to a result or to a circumstance described by a statute defining an offense when he fails to perceive a substantial and unjustifiable risk that such result will occur or that such circumstance exists. The risk must be of such nature and degree that the failure to perceive it constitutes a gross deviation from the standard of care that a reasonable person would observe in the situation;

(15) "Machine gun" means a weapon of any description, irrespective of size, by whatever name known, loaded or unloaded, from which a number of shots or bullets may be rapidly or automatically discharged from a magazine with one continuous pull of the trigger and includes a submachine gun;

(16) "Rifle" means a weapon designed or redesigned, made or remade, and intended to be fired from the shoulder and designed or redesigned and made or remade to use the energy of the explosive in a fixed metallic cartridge to fire only a single projectile through a rifled bore for each single pull of the trigger;

(17) "Shotgun" means a weapon designed or redesigned, made or remade, and intended to be fired from the shoulder and designed or redesigned and made or remade to use the energy of the explosive in a fixed shotgun shell to fire through a smooth bore either a number of ball shot or a single projectile for each single pull of the trigger;

(18) "Pistol" or "revolver" means any firearm having a barrel less than twelve inches;

(19) "Firearm" means any sawed-off shotgun, machine gun, rifle, shotgun, pistol, revolver or other weapon, whether loaded or unloaded from which a shot may be discharged;

(20) "Electronic defense weapon" means a weapon which by electronic impulse or current is capable of immobilizing a person temporarily, but is not capable of inflicting death or serious physical injury;

(21) "Martial arts weapon" means a nunchaku, kama, kasari-fundo, octagon sai, tonfa or chinese star;

(22) "Employee of an emergency medical service organization" means an ambulance driver, emergency medical technician or paramedic as defined in section 19a-175;

APPENDIX B

(23) "Railroad property" means all tangible property owned, leased or operated by a railroad carrier including, but not limited to, a right-of-way, track, roadbed, bridge, yard, shop, station, tunnel, viaduct, trestle, depot, warehouse, terminal or any other structure or appurtenance or equipment owned, leased or used in the operation of a railroad carrier including a train, locomotive, engine, railroad car, signals or safety device or work equipment or rolling stock.

Sec. 21a-240. (Formerly Sec. 19-443). Definitions. The following words and phrases, as used in this chapter, shall have the following meanings, unless the context otherwise requires:

(1) "Abuse of drugs" means the use of controlled substances solely for their stimulant, depressant or hallucinogenic effect upon the higher functions of the central nervous system and not as a therapeutic agent prescribed in the course of medical treatment or in a program of research operated under the direction of a physician or pharmacologist;

(2) "Administer" means the direct application of a controlled substance, whether by injection, inhalation, ingestion or any other means, to the body of a patient or research subject by: (A) A practitioner, or, in his presence, by his authorized agent, or (B) the patient or research subject at the direction and in the presence of the practitioner, or (C) a nurse or intern under the direction and supervision of a practitioner;

(3) "Agent" means an authorized person who acts on behalf of or at the direction of a manufacturer, distributor or dispenser. It does not include a common or contract carrier, public warehouseman, or employee of the carrier or warehouseman;

(4) "Amphetamine-type substances" include amphetamine, optical isomers thereof, salts of amphetamine and its isomers, and chemical compounds which are similar thereto in chemical structure or which are similar thereto in physiological effect, and which show a like potential for abuse, which are controlled substances under this chapter unless modified;

(5) "Barbiturate-type drugs" include barbituric acid and its salts, derivatives thereof and chemical compounds which are similar thereto in chemical structure or which are similar thereto in physiological effect, and which show a like potential for abuse, which are controlled substances under this chapter unless modified;

(6) "Bureau" means the Bureau of Narcotics and Dangerous Drugs, United States Department of Justice, or its successor agency;

(7) "Cannabis-type substances" include all parts of any plant, or species of the genus cannabis or any infra specific taxon thereof whether growing or not; the seeds thereof; the resin extracted from any part of such a plant; and every compound, manufacture, salt, derivative, mixture or preparation of such plant, its seeds or resin; but shall not include the mature stalks of such plant, fiber produced from such stalks, oil or cake made from the seeds of such plant, any other compound, manufacture, salt, derivative, mixture or preparation of such mature stalks, except the resin extracted therefrom, fiber, oil or cake, or the sterilized seed of such plant which is incapable of germination. Included are cannabinon, cannabinol, cannabidiol and chemical compounds which are similar to cannabinon, cannabinol or cannabidiol in chemical structure or which are similar thereto in physiological effect, and which show a like potential for abuse, which are controlled substances under this chapter unless modified;

(8) "Controlled drugs" are those drugs which contain any quantity of a substance which has been designated as subject to the federal Controlled Substances Act, or which has been designated as a depressant or stimulant drug pursuant to federal food and drug laws, or which has been designated by the Commissioner of Consumer Protection pursuant to section 21a-243, as having a stimulant, depressant or hallucinogenic effect upon the higher functions of the central nervous system and as having a tendency to promote abuse or psychological or physiological dependence, or both. Such controlled drugs are classifiable as amphetamine-type, barbiturate-type, cannabis-type, cocaine-type, hallucinogenic, morphine-type and other stimulant and depressant drugs. Specifically excluded from controlled drugs and controlled substances are alcohol, nicotine and caffeine;

(9) "Controlled substance" means a drug, substance, or immediate precursor in schedules I to V, inclusive, of the Connecticut controlled substance scheduling regulations adopted pursuant to section 21a-243;

(10) "Counterfeit substance" means a controlled substance which, or the container or labeling of which, without authorization, bears the trademark, trade name or other identifying mark, imprint, number or device, or any likeness thereof, of a manufacturer, distributor or dispenser other than the person who in fact manufactured, distributed or dispensed the substance;

(11) "Deliver or delivery" means the actual, constructive or attempted transfer from one person to another of a controlled substance, whether or not there is an agency relationship;

(12) "Dentist" means a person authorized by law to practice dentistry in this state;

(13) "Dispense" means to deliver a controlled substance to an ultimate user or research subject by or pursuant to the lawful order of a practitioner, including the prescribing, administering, packaging, labeling or compounding necessary to prepare the substance for the delivery;

(14) "Dispenser" means a practitioner who dispenses;

(15) "Distribute" means to deliver other than by administering or dispensing a controlled substance;

(16) "Distributor" means a person who distributes and includes a wholesaler who is a person supplying or distributing controlled drugs which he himself has not produced or prepared to hospitals, clinics, practitioners, pharmacies, other wholesalers, manufacturers and federal, state and municipal agencies;

(17) "Drug" means (A) substances recognized as drugs in the official United States Pharmacopoeia, official Homeopathic Pharmacopoeia of the United States, or official National Formulary, or any supplement to any of them; (B) substances intended for use in the diagnosis, cure, mitigation, treatment or prevention of disease in man or animals; (C) substances, other than food, intended to affect the structure or any function of the body of man or animals; and (D) substances intended for use as a component of any article specified in subparagraph (A), (B) or (C) of this subdivision. It does not include devices or their components, parts or accessories;

APPENDIX B

(18) "Drug dependence" means a psychoactive substance dependence on drugs as that condition is defined in the most recent edition of the "Diagnostic and Statistical Manual of Mental Disorders" of the American Psychiatric Association;

(19) "Drug-dependent person" means a person who has a psychoactive substance dependence on drugs as that condition is defined in the most recent edition of the "Diagnostic and Statistical Manual of Mental Disorders" of the American Psychiatric Association;

(20) (A) "Drug paraphernalia" refers to equipment, products and materials of any kind which are used, intended for use or designed for use in planting, propagating, cultivating, growing, harvesting, manufacturing, compounding, converting, producing, processing, preparing, testing, analyzing, packaging, repackaging, storing, containing or concealing, or ingesting, inhaling or otherwise introducing into the human body, any controlled substance contrary to the provisions of this chapter including, but not limited to: (i) Kits intended for use or designed for use in planting, propagating, cultivating, growing or harvesting of any species of plant which is a controlled substance or from which a controlled substance can be derived; (ii) kits used, intended for use or designed for use in manufacturing, compounding, converting, producing, processing or preparing controlled substances; (iii) isomerization devices used, intended for use in increasing the potency of any species of plant which is a controlled substance; (iv) testing equipment used, intended for use or designed for use in identifying or analyzing the strength, effectiveness or purity of controlled substances; (v) dilutents and adulterants, such as quinine hydrochloride, mannitol, mannite, dextrose and lactose used, intended for use or designed for use in cutting controlled substances; (vi) separation gins and sifters used, intended for use or designed for use in removing twigs and seeds from, or in otherwise cleaning or refining, marijuana; (vii) capsules and other containers used, intended for use or designed for use in packaging small quantities of controlled substances; (viii) containers and other objects used, intended for use or designed for use in storing or concealing controlled substances; (ix) objects used, intended for use or designed for use in ingesting, inhaling, or otherwise introducing marijuana, cocaine, hashish, or hashish oil into the human body, such as: Metal, wooden, acrylic, glass, stone, plastic or ceramic pipes with screens, permanent screens, hashish heads or punctured metal bowls; water pipes; carburetion tubes and devices; smoking and carburetion masks; roach clips: Meaning objects used to hold burning material, such as a marijuana cigarette, that has become too small or too short to be held in the hand; miniature cocaine spoons, and cocaine vials; chamber pipes; carburetor pipes; electric pipes; air-driven pipes; chillums; bongs or ice pipes or chillers;

(B) "Factory" means any place used for the manufacturing, mixing, compounding, refining, processing, packaging, distributing, storing, keeping, holding, administering or assembling illegal substances contrary to the provisions of this chapter, or any building, rooms or location which contains equipment or paraphernalia used for this purpose;

(21) "Federal Controlled Substances Act, 21 USC 801 et seq." means Public Law 91-513, the Comprehensive Drug Abuse Prevention and Control Act of 1970;

(22) "Federal food and drug laws" means the federal Food, Drug and Cosmetic Act, as amended, Title 21 USC 301 et seq.;

(23) "Hallucinogenic substances" are psychodysleptic substances which assert a confusional or disorganizing effect upon mental processes or behavior and mimic acute psychotic

disturbances. Exemplary of such drugs are mescaline, peyote, psilocyn and d-lysergic acid diethylamide, which are controlled substances under this chapter unless modified;

(24) "Hospital," as used in sections 21a-243 to 21a-283, inclusive, means an institution for the care and treatment of the sick and injured, approved by the Department of Public Health or the Department of Mental Health and Addiction Services as proper to be entrusted with the custody of controlled drugs and substances and professional use of controlled drugs and substances under the direction of a licensed practitioner;

(25) "Intern" means a person who holds a degree of doctor of medicine or doctor of dental surgery or medicine and whose period of service has been recorded with the Department of Public Health and who has been accepted and is participating in training by a hospital or institution in this state. Doctors meeting the foregoing requirements and commonly designated as "residents" and "fellows" shall be regarded as interns for purposes of this chapter;

(26) "Immediate precursor" means a substance which the Commissioner of Consumer Protection has found to be, and by regulation designates as being, the principal compound commonly used or produced primarily for use, and which is an immediate chemical intermediary used or likely to be used, in the manufacture of a controlled substance, the control of which is necessary to prevent, curtail or limit manufacture;

(27) "Laboratory" means a laboratory approved by the Department of Consumer Protection as proper to be entrusted with the custody of controlled substances and the use of controlled substances for scientific and medical purposes and for purposes of instruction, research or analysis;

(28) "Manufacture" means the production, preparation, cultivation, growing, propagation, compounding, conversion or processing of a controlled substance, either directly or indirectly by extraction from substances of natural origin, or independently by means of chemical synthesis, or by a combination of extraction and chemical synthesis, and includes any packaging or repackaging of the substance or labeling or relabeling of its container, except that this term does not include the preparation or compounding of a controlled substance by an individual for his own use or the preparation, compounding, packaging or labeling of a controlled substance: (A) By a practitioner as an incident to his administering or dispensing of a controlled substance in the course of his professional practice, or (B) by a practitioner, or by his authorized agent under his supervision, for the purpose of, or as an incident to, research, teaching or chemical analysis and not for sale;

(29) "Marijuana" means all parts of any plant, or species of the genus cannabis or any infra specific taxon thereof, whether growing or not; the seeds thereof; the resin extracted from any part of the plant; and every compound, manufacture, salt, derivative, mixture, or preparation of such plant, its seeds or resin. It does not include the mature stalks of such plant, fiber produced from such stalks, oil or cake made from the seeds of such plant, any other compound, manufacture, salt, derivative, mixture or preparation of such mature stalks, except the resin extracted therefrom, fiber, oil, or cake, or the sterilized seed of such plant which is incapable of germination. Included are cannabinon, cannabinol or cannabidiol and chemical compounds which are similar to cannabinon, cannabinol or cannabidiol in chemical structure or which are similar thereto in physiological effect, and which show a like potential for abuse, which are controlled substances under this chapter unless modified;

APPENDIX B

(30) "Narcotic substance" means any of the following, whether produced directly or indirectly by extraction from substances of vegetable origin, or independently by means of chemical synthesis, or by a combination of extraction and chemical synthesis: (A) Morphine-type: (i) Opium and opiate, and any salt, compound, derivative, or preparation of opium or opiate which are similar thereto in chemical structure or which are similar thereto in physiological effect and which show a like potential for abuse, which are controlled substances under this chapter unless modified; (ii) any salt, compound, isomer, derivative, or preparation thereof which is chemically equivalent or identical with any of the substances referred to in clause (i), but not including the isoquinoline alkaloids of opium; (iii) opium poppy and poppy straw; (B) cocaine-type, coca leaves and any salt, compound, derivative or preparation of coca leaves, and any salt, compound, isomer, derivatives or preparation thereof which is chemically equivalent or identical with any of these substances or which are similar thereto in physiological effect and which show a like potential for abuse, but not including decocainized coca leaves or extractions of coca leaves which do not contain cocaine or ecgonine;

(31) "Nurse" means a person performing nursing as defined in section 20-87a;

(32) "Official written order" means an order for controlled substances written on a form provided by the bureau for that purpose under the federal Controlled Substances Act;

(33) "Opiate" means any substance having an addiction-forming or addiction-sustaining liability similar to morphine or being capable of conversion into a drug having addiction-forming or addiction-sustaining liability; it does not include, unless specifically designated as controlled under this chapter, the dextrorotatory isomer of 3-methoxy-n-methylmorthinan and its salts (dextro-methorphan) but shall include its racemic and levorotatory forms;

(34) "Opium poppy" means the plant of the species papaver somniferum l., except its seed;

(35) Repealed by P.A. 99-102, S. 51;

(36) "Other stimulant and depressant drugs" means controlled substances other than amphetamine-type, barbiturate-type, cannabis-type, cocaine-type, hallucinogenics and morphine-type which are found to exert a stimulant and depressant effect upon the higher functions of the central nervous system and which are found to have a potential for abuse and are controlled substances under this chapter;

(37) "Person" includes any corporation, limited liability company, association or partnership, or one or more individuals, government or governmental subdivisions or agency, business trust, estate, trust, or any other legal entity. Words importing the plural number may include the singular; words importing the masculine gender may be applied to females;

(38) "Pharmacist" means a person authorized by law to practice pharmacy pursuant to section 20-590, 20-591, 20-592 or 20-593;

(39) "Pharmacy" means an establishment licensed pursuant to section 20-594;

(40) "Physician" means a person authorized by law to practice medicine in this state pursuant to section 20-9;

(41) "Podiatrist" means a person authorized by law to practice podiatry in this state;

(42) "Poppy straw" means all parts, except the seeds, of the opium poppy, after mowing;

(43) "Practitioner" means: (A) A physician, dentist, veterinarian, podiatrist, scientific investigator or other person licensed, registered or otherwise permitted to distribute, dispense, conduct research with respect to or to administer a controlled substance in the course of professional practice or research in this state; (B) a pharmacy, hospital or other institution licensed, registered or otherwise permitted to distribute, dispense, conduct research with respect to or to administer a controlled substance in the course of professional practice or research in this state;

(44) "Prescribe" means order or designate a remedy or any preparation containing controlled substances;

(45) "Prescription" means a written, oral or electronic order for any controlled substance or preparation from a licensed practitioner to a pharmacist for a patient;

(46) "Production" includes the manufacture, planting, cultivation, growing or harvesting of a controlled substance;

(47) "Registrant" means any person licensed by this state and assigned a current federal Bureau of Narcotics and Dangerous Drug Registry Number as provided under the federal Controlled Substances Act;

(48) "Registry number" means the alphabetical or numerical designation of identification assigned to a person by the federal Drug Enforcement Administration, or other federal agency, which is commonly known as the federal registry number;

(49) "Restricted drugs or substances" are the following substances without limitation and for all purposes: Datura stramonium; hyoscyamus niger; atropa belladonna, or the alkaloids atropine; hyoscyamine; belladonnine; apatropine; or any mixture of these alkaloids such as daturine, or the synthetic homatropine or any salts of these alkaloids, except that any drug or preparation containing any of the above-mentioned substances which is permitted by federal food and drug laws to be sold or dispensed without a prescription or written order shall not be a controlled substance; amyl nitrite; the following volatile substances to the extent that said chemical substances or compounds containing said chemical substances are sold, prescribed, dispensed, compounded, possessed or controlled or delivered or administered to another person with the purpose that said chemical substances shall be breathed, inhaled, sniffed or drunk to induce a stimulant, depressant or hallucinogenic effect upon the higher functions of the central nervous system: Acetone; benzene; butyl alcohol; butyl nitrate and its salts, isomers, esters, ethers or their salts; cyclohexanone; dichlorodifluoromethane; ether; ethyl acetate; formaldehyde; hexane; isopropanol; methanol; methyl cellosolve acetate; methyl ethyl ketone; methyl isobutyl ketone; nitrous oxide; pentochlorophenol; toluene; toluol; trichloroethane; trichloroethylene; 1,4 butanediol;

(50) "Sale" is any form of delivery which includes barter, exchange or gift, or offer therefor, and each such transaction made by any person whether as principal, proprietor, agent, servant or employee;

(51) "State," when applied to a part of the United States, includes any state, district, commonwealth, territory or insular possession thereof, and any area subject to the legal authority of the United States of America;

(52) "State food, drug and cosmetic laws" means the Uniform Food, Drug and Cosmetic Act, section 21a-91 et seq.;

(53) "Ultimate user" means a person who lawfully possesses a controlled substance for his own use or for the use of a member of his household or for administering to an animal owned by him or by a member of his household;

(54) "Veterinarian" means a person authorized by law to practice veterinary medicine in this state;

(55) "Wholesaler" means a distributor or a person who supplies controlled substances that he himself has not produced or prepared to registrants as defined in subdivision (47) of this section;

(56) "Reasonable times" means the time or times any office, care-giving institution, pharmacy, clinic, wholesaler, manufacturer, laboratory, warehouse, establishment, store or place of business, vehicle or other place is open for the normal affairs or business or the practice activities usually conducted by the registrant;

(57) "Unit dose drug distribution system" means a drug distribution system used in a hospital or chronic and convalescent nursing home in which drugs are supplied in individually labeled unit of use packages, each patient's supply of drugs is exchanged between the hospital pharmacy and the drug administration area or, in the case of a chronic and convalescent nursing home between a pharmacy and the drug administration area, at least once each twenty-four hours and each patient's medication supply for this period is stored within a patient-specific container, all of which is conducted under the direction of a pharmacist licensed in Connecticut and, in the case of a hospital, directly involved in the provision and supervision of pharmaceutical services at such hospital at least thirty-five hours each week;

(58) "Cocaine in a free-base form" means any substance which contains cocaine, or any compound, isomer, derivative or preparation thereof, in a nonsalt form.

Sec. 1-210. (Formerly Sec. 1-19). Access to public records. Exempt records.
(a) Except as otherwise provided by any federal law or state statute, all records maintained or kept on file by any public agency, whether or not such records are required by any law or by any rule or regulation, shall be public records and every person shall have the right to (1) inspect such records promptly during regular office or business hours, (2) copy such records in accordance with subsection (g) of section 1-212, or (3) receive a copy of such records in accordance with section 1-212. Any agency rule or regulation, or part thereof, that conflicts with the provisions of this subsection or diminishes or curtails in any way the rights granted by this subsection shall be void. Each such agency shall keep and maintain all public records in its custody at its regular office or place of business in an accessible place and, if there is no such office or place of business, the public records pertaining to such agency shall be kept in the office of the clerk of the political subdivision in which such public agency is located or of the Secretary

of the State, as the case may be. Any certified record hereunder attested as a true copy by the clerk, chief or deputy of such agency or by such other person designated or empowered by law to so act, shall be competent evidence in any court of this state of the facts contained therein.

(b) Nothing in the Freedom of Information Act shall be construed to require disclosure of:

(1) Preliminary drafts or notes provided the public agency has determined that the public interest in withholding such documents clearly outweighs the public interest in disclosure;

(2) Personnel or medical files and similar files the disclosure of which would constitute an invasion of personal privacy;

(3) Records of law enforcement agencies not otherwise available to the public which records were compiled in connection with the detection or investigation of crime, if the disclosure of said records would not be in the public interest because it would result in the disclosure of (A) the identity of informants not otherwise known or the identity of witnesses not otherwise known whose safety would be endangered or who would be subject to threat or intimidation if their identity was made known, (B) the identity of minor witnesses, (C) signed statements of witnesses, (D) information to be used in a prospective law enforcement action if prejudicial to such action, (E) investigatory techniques not otherwise known to the general public, (F) arrest records of a juvenile, which shall also include any investigatory files, concerning the arrest of such juvenile, compiled for law enforcement purposes, (G) the name and address of the victim of a sexual assault under section 53a-70, 53a-70a, 53a-71, 53a-72a, 53a-72b or 53a-73a, voyeurism under section 53a-189a, or injury or risk of injury, or impairing of morals under section 53-21, or of an attempt thereof, or (H) uncorroborated allegations subject to destruction pursuant to section 1-216;

(4) Records pertaining to strategy and negotiations with respect to pending claims or pending litigation to which the public agency is a party until such litigation or claim has been finally adjudicated or otherwise settled;

(5) (A) Trade secrets, which for purposes of the Freedom of Information Act, are defined as information, including formulas, patterns, compilations, programs, devices, methods, techniques, processes, drawings, cost data, customer lists, film or television scripts or detailed production budgets that (i) derive independent economic value, actual or potential, from not being generally known to, and not being readily ascertainable by proper means by, other persons who can obtain economic value from their disclosure or use, and (ii) are the subject of efforts that are reasonable under the circumstances to maintain secrecy; and

(B) Commercial or financial information given in confidence, not required by statute;

(6) Test questions, scoring keys and other examination data used to administer a licensing examination, examination for employment or academic examinations;

(7) The contents of real estate appraisals, engineering or feasibility estimates and evaluations made for or by an agency relative to the acquisition of property or to prospective public supply and construction contracts, until such time as all of the property has been acquired or all proceedings or transactions have been terminated or abandoned, provided the law of eminent domain shall not be affected by this provision;

APPENDIX B

(8) Statements of personal worth or personal financial data required by a licensing agency and filed by an applicant with such licensing agency to establish the applicant's personal qualification for the license, certificate or permit applied for;

(9) Records, reports and statements of strategy or negotiations with respect to collective bargaining;

(10) Records, tax returns, reports and statements exempted by federal law or the general statutes or communications privileged by the attorney-client relationship, marital relationship, clergy-penitent relationship, doctor-patient relationship, therapist-patient relationship or any other privilege established by the common law or the general statutes, including any such records, tax returns, reports or communications that were created or made prior to the establishment of the applicable privilege under the common law or the general statutes

(11) Names or addresses of students enrolled in any public school or college without the consent of each student whose name or address is to be disclosed who is eighteen years of age or older and a parent or guardian of each such student who is younger than eighteen years of age, provided this subdivision shall not be construed as prohibiting the disclosure of the names or addresses of students enrolled in any public school in a regional school district to the board of selectmen or town board of finance, as the case may be, of the town wherein the student resides for the purpose of verifying tuition payments made to such school;

(12) Any information obtained by the use of illegal means;

(13) Records of an investigation or the name of an employee providing information under the provisions of section 4-61dd or sections 4-276 to 4-280, inclusive;

(14) Adoption records and information provided for in sections 45a-746, 45a-750 and 45a-751;

(15) Any page of a primary petition, nominating petition, referendum petition or petition for a town meeting submitted under any provision of the general statutes or of any special act, municipal charter or ordinance, until the required processing and certification of such page has been completed by the official or officials charged with such duty after which time disclosure of such page shall be required;

(16) Records of complaints, including information compiled in the investigation thereof, brought to a municipal health authority pursuant to chapter 368e or a district department of health pursuant to chapter 368f, until such time as the investigation is concluded or thirty days from the date of receipt of the complaint, whichever occurs first;

(17) Educational records which are not subject to disclosure under the Family Educational Rights and Privacy Act, 20 USC 1232g;

(18) Records, the disclosure of which the Commissioner of Correction, or as it applies to Whiting Forensic Division facilities of the Connecticut Valley Hospital, the Commissioner of Mental Health and Addiction Services, has reasonable grounds to believe may result in a safety risk, including the risk of harm to any person or the risk of an escape from, or a disorder

in, a correctional institution or facility under the supervision of the Department of Correction or Whiting Forensic Division facilities. Such records shall include, but are not limited to:

(A) Security manuals, including emergency plans contained or referred to in such security manuals;

(B) Engineering and architectural drawings of correctional institutions or facilities or Whiting Forensic Division facilities;

(C) Operational specifications of security systems utilized by the Department of Correction at any correctional institution or facility or Whiting Forensic Division facilities, except that a general description of any such security system and the cost and quality of such system may be disclosed;

(D) Training manuals prepared for correctional institutions and facilities or Whiting Forensic Division facilities that describe, in any manner, security procedures, emergency plans or security equipment;

(E) Internal security audits of correctional institutions and facilities or Whiting Forensic Division facilities;

(F) Minutes or recordings of staff meetings of the Department of Correction or Whiting Forensic Division facilities, or portions of such minutes or recordings, that contain or reveal information relating to security or other records otherwise exempt from disclosure under this subdivision;

(G) Logs or other documents that contain information on the movement or assignment of inmates or staff at correctional institutions or facilities; and

(H) Records that contain information on contacts between inmates, as defined in section 18-84, and law enforcement officers;

(19) Records when there are reasonable grounds to believe disclosure may result in a safety risk, including the risk of harm to any person, any government-owned or leased institution or facility or any fixture or appurtenance and equipment attached to, or contained in, such institution or facility, except that such records shall be disclosed to a law enforcement agency upon the request of the law enforcement agency. Such reasonable grounds shall be determined (A) (i) by the Commissioner of Administrative Services, after consultation with the chief executive officer of an executive branch state agency, with respect to records concerning such agency; and (ii) by the Commissioner of Emergency Services and Public Protection, after consultation with the chief executive officer of a municipal, district or regional agency, with respect to records concerning such agency; (B) by the Chief Court Administrator with respect to records concerning the Judicial Department; and (C) by the executive director of the Joint Committee on Legislative Management, with respect to records concerning the Legislative Department. As used in this section, "government-owned or leased institution or facility" includes, but is not limited to, an institution or facility owned or leased by a public service company, as defined in section 16-1, a certified telecommunications provider, as defined in section 16-1, a water company, as defined in section 25-32a, or a municipal utility that fur-

nishes electric, gas or water service, but does not include an institution or facility owned or leased by the federal government, and "chief executive officer" includes, but is not limited to, an agency head, department head, executive director or chief executive officer. Such records include, but are not limited to:

(i) Security manuals or reports;

(ii) Engineering and architectural drawings of government-owned or leased institutions or facilities;

(iii) Operational specifications of security systems utilized at any government-owned or leased institution or facility, except that a general description of any such security system and the cost and quality of such system, may be disclosed;

(iv) Training manuals prepared for government-owned or leased institutions or facilities that describe, in any manner, security procedures, emergency plans or security equipment;

(v) Internal security audits of government-owned or leased institutions or facilities;

(vi) Minutes or records of meetings, or portions of such minutes or records, that contain or reveal information relating to security or other records otherwise exempt from disclosure under this subdivision;

(vii) Logs or other documents that contain information on the movement or assignment of security personnel;

(viii) Emergency plans and emergency preparedness, response, recovery and mitigation plans, including plans provided by a person to a state agency or a local emergency management agency or official; and

(ix) With respect to a water company, as defined in section 25-32a, that provides water service: Vulnerability assessments and risk management plans, operational plans, portions of water supply plans submitted pursuant to section 25-32d that contain or reveal information the disclosure of which may result in a security risk to a water company, inspection reports, technical specifications and other materials that depict or specifically describe critical water company operating facilities, collection and distribution systems or sources of supply;

(20) Records of standards, procedures, processes, software and codes, not otherwise available to the public, the disclosure of which would compromise the security or integrity of an information technology system;

(21) The residential, work or school address of any participant in the address confidentiality program established pursuant to sections 54-240 to 54-240o, inclusive;

(22) The electronic mail address of any person that is obtained by the Department of Transportation in connection with the implementation or administration of any plan to inform individuals about significant highway or railway incidents;

(23) The name or address of any minor enrolled in any parks and recreation program administered or sponsored by any public agency;

(24) Responses to any request for proposals or bid solicitation issued by a public agency or any record or file made by a public agency in connection with the contract award process, until such contract is executed or negotiations for the award of such contract have ended, whichever occurs earlier, provided the chief executive officer of such public agency certifies that the public interest in the disclosure of such responses, record or file is outweighed by the public interest in the confidentiality of such responses, record or file;

(25) The name, address, telephone number or electronic mail address of any person enrolled in any senior center program or any member of a senior center administered or sponsored by any public agency.

(26) All records obtained during the course of inspection, investigation, examination and audit activities of an institution, as defined in section 19a-490, that are confidential pursuant to a contract between the Department of Public Health and the United States Department of Health and Human Services relating to the Medicare and Medicaid programs;

(27) Any record created by a law enforcement agency or other federal, state, or municipal governmental agency consisting of a photograph, film, video or digital or other visual image depicting the victim of a homicide, to the extent that such record could reasonably be expected to constitute an unwarranted invasion of the personal privacy of the victim or the victim's surviving family members.

(c) Whenever a public agency receives a request from any person confined in a correctional institution or facility or a Whiting Forensic Division facility, for disclosure of any public record under the Freedom of Information Act, the public agency shall promptly notify the Commissioner of Correction or the Commissioner of Mental Health and Addiction Services in the case of a person confined in a Whiting Forensic Division facility of such request, in the manner prescribed by the commissioner, before complying with the request as required by the Freedom of Information Act. If the commissioner believes the requested record is exempt from disclosure pursuant to subdivision (18) of subsection (b) of this section, the commissioner may withhold such record from such person when the record is delivered to the person's correctional institution or facility or Whiting Forensic Division facility.

(d) Whenever a public agency, except the Judicial Department or Legislative Department, receives a request from any person for disclosure of any records described in subdivision (19) of subsection (b) of this section under the Freedom of Information Act, the public agency shall promptly notify the Commissioner of Administrative Services or the Commissioner of Emergency Services and Public Protection, as applicable, of such request, in the manner prescribed by such commissioner, before complying with the request as required by the Freedom of Information Act and for information related to a water company, as defined in section 25-32a, the public agency shall promptly notify the water company before complying with the request as required by the Freedom of Information Act. If the commissioner, after consultation with the chief executive officer of the applicable agency or after consultation with the chief executive officer of the applicable water company for information related to a water company, as defined in section 25-32a, believes the requested record is exempt from disclosure pursuant to subdivision (19) of subsection (b) of this section, the commissioner may direct the agency to withhold such record from such person. In any appeal brought under the provisions of section 1-206 of the Freedom of Information Act for denial of access to records for any of the reasons described in subdivision (19) of subsection (b) of this section, such appeal shall be against the chief executive officer of the executive branch state agency or the municipal, district or regional agency that issued the directive to withhold such record pursuant to subdivision (19) of subsection (b) of this section, exclusively, or, in the case of records concerning Judicial Department facilities, the Chief Court Administrator or, in the case of records concerning the Legislative Department, the executive director of the Joint Committee on Legislative Management.

(e) Notwithstanding the provisions of subdivisions (1) and (16) of subsection (b) of this section, disclosure shall be required of:

(1) Interagency or intra-agency memoranda or letters, advisory opinions, recommendations or any report comprising part of the process by which governmental decisions and policies are formulated, except disclosure shall not be required of a preliminary draft of a memorandum, prepared by a member of the staff of a public agency, which is subject to revision prior to submission to or discussion among the members of such agency;

(2) All records of investigation conducted with respect to any tenement house, lodging house or boarding house as defined in section 19a-355, or any nursing home, residential care home or rest home, as defined in section 19a-490, by any municipal building department or housing code inspection department, any local or district health department, or any other department charged with the enforcement of ordinances or laws regulating the erection, construction, alteration, maintenance, sanitation, ventilation or occupancy of such buildings; and

(3) The names of firms obtaining bid documents from any state agency.

CT Gen Stat § 1-200 (2013)
As used in this chapter, the following words and phrases shall have the following meanings, except where such terms are used in a context which clearly indicates the contrary:

(6) "Executive sessions" means a meeting of a public agency at which the public is excluded for one or more of the following purposes: (A) Discussion concerning the appointment, employment, performance, evaluation, health or dismissal of a public officer or employee, provided that such individual may require that discussion be held at an open meeting; (B) strategy and negotiations with respect to pending claims or pending litigation to which the public agency or a member thereof, because of the member's conduct as a member of such agency, is a party until such litigation or claim has been finally adjudicated or otherwise settled; (C) matters concerning security strategy or the deployment of security personnel, or devices affecting public security; (D) discussion of the selection of a site or the lease, sale or purchase of real estate by the state or a political subdivision of the state when publicity regarding such site, lease, sale, purchase or construction would adversely impact the price of such site, lease, sale, purchase or construction until such time as all of the property has been acquired or all proceedings or transactions concerning same have been terminated or abandoned; and (E) discussion of any matter which would result in the disclosure of public records or the information contained therein described in subsection (b) of section 1-210.

www.ingramcontent.com/pod-product-compliance
Lightning Source LLC
Chambersburg PA
CBHW070550300426
44113CB00011B/1847